Making Homemade CHEESES & BUTTER

by PHYLLIS HOBSON

A Garden Way Guide
of HOMESTEAD RECIPES

GARDEN WAY PUBLISHING
CHARLOTTE, VERMONT, 05445

Library of Congress Catalog Card Number: 73-89125

ISBN 0-88266-019-5

COPYRIGHT 1973 BY GARDEN WAY PUBLISHING CO.

Fifth printing, November, 1975

Designed by Frank Lieberman

PRINTED IN THE UNITED STATES

CONTENTS

MAKING YOUR OWN CHEESE

If you have a couple of goats or a cow on your homestead, (and if you haven't you're missing one of the most satisfying aspects of country life), you're sure to find yourself with several gallons of surplus milk on hand. Few families, even those with several milk drinkers, can keep up with the output of a good cow on green pasture, and most goats will average a gallon of milk a day during the summer months.

You can make butter and buttermilk, of course. We've included a couple of good recipes and a method of skimming milk without a cream separator. You can make yogurt according to the recipe on Page 36. You can freeze packages of butter or cartons of whole milk (Page 33) for the less bountiful winter months. You even may want to can the milk. There's a recipe on Page 39.

But the best solution to a surplus of milk is cheese — the most delicious, nutritious method of preserving milk yet devised. Cheese contains all the nutrients of milk in concentrated form. One pound of hard cheese contains most of the protein, calcium, riboflavin and Vitamin A of one gallon of milk. In addition, the curing process increases the B vitamins.

It isn't feasible to make cheese in very small batches because the curing process is not satisfactory in cheeses less than one pound in size. You may have to "save up" for a week or more to have enough surplus milk to make a batch of cheese, but this works out well if you keep the milk refrigerated.

However, once you get used to the idea of working with three or four gallons of milk, making cheese in these comparatively small quantities is a simple process easily adapted to the homestead kitchen. Few ingredients are needed, and most of the necessary equipment is already on hand. The rest can be fabricated in the home workshop.

The instructions for making cheese sound complicated, but the process is really much simpler than baking a cake. For each recipe read the Basic Directions through first, then the specific recipe. Then read each step carefully as you go. With only a little practice you can become a cheese-making expert.

As you gain confidence you will learn the variables of cheese making — the degree of ripening of the milk and its effect on the flavor, the length of time the curd is heated and how it affects the texture, the amount of salt, the number of bricks used in pressing and the effect on moisture content, and how long the cheese is cured for sharpness of taste. All of these variables affect the finished product and produce the many varieties of flavor and texture. The more you learn about it, the more fascinating cheese-making becomes. There are three kinds of cheese — Hard, Soft and Cottage. Here are recipes for all three:

HARD CHEESE Hard Cheese is the curd of milk (the white, solid portion) separated from the whey (the watery, clear liquid). Once separated, the curd is pressed into a solid cake and aged for flavor. Well-pressed, well-aged cheese will keep for months. Most hard cheeses can be eaten immediately but are better flavored if they are aged. The longer the aging period, the sharper the flavor. The heavier the pressing weight, the harder the texture. Hard cheese is best when made of whole milk.

SOFT CHEESE Soft cheese is made in the same way, but is pressed just long enough to retain its shape. It is not paraffined and is aged a short time or not at all. Most soft cheeses can be eaten immediately and are best eaten within two to three weeks. Cheeses such as Camembert, Gorgonzola and Roquefort are soft cheeses which have been put aside to cure. They do not keep as long as hard cheeses because of their higher moisture content. Soft cheese may be made of whole or skim milk.

COTTAGE CHEESE Cottage cheese is a soft, uncured spoon cheese prepared from a high-moisture curd that is not allowed to cure. Commercially it usually is made of skim milk, but it can be made of whole milk. Cottage cheese is the simplest of all cheeses to make. The fresh (or warmed) milk is allowed to stand until a thick clabber is formed or is cultured by adding a starter or buttermilk or sour milk. We often use yogurt. The clabbered milk is heated slightly to separate the curd from the whey. The curd is strained out, mixed with butter and made into cheese balls for spreading or is mixed with cream and is used as a soft spoon cheese.

YOU'LL NEED:

The list is long, but don't let that scare you off. Most of the necessary utensils already are in your kitchen. The rest can be put together in a few minutes with a coffee can and a few boards.

A Cheese Form — Make your own from a two-pound coffee can by punching nail holes in the bottom. Be sure to punch the holes from the inside out so the rough edges are on the outside of the can and will not tear the cheese. The cheese form is lined with cheesecloth and filled with the wet curd, which then is covered with another piece of cheesecloth before the follower is inserted for pressing.

The excess whey drains from the curd through the nail holes in the can.

A Follower — This is a round piece of wood, ½ to 1 inch thick and just enough smaller in diameter than the coffee can that it can be inserted inside and moved up and down easily. The follower forces the wet curd together, forming a solid cake and squeezing out the whey.

A Cheese Press — An old fashioned lard press works fine once you learn how much pressure to exert. They're considered collectors' items, but you can still buy them at farm auctions for less than $10. You can make a cheese press in an afternoon with 50 cents worth of wood and a broom stick handle. If you plan to make hard cheese regularly, it will be worth the time or money to buy a lard press or construct a good wooden cheese press.

But if you make cheese once or twice a year, you can improvise with a coffee can cheese form, a follower and some bricks. Chr. Hansen Laboratory, Inc., 9015 W. Maple St., Milwaukee, Wis. 53214 markets a good simple press.

A Container — We use two hot water canners, double boiler style, placing one inside the other. We recommend them because they are lightweight (4 gallons of milk can get heavy), they are porcelain enamel-covered (aluminum is affected by the acid in the curd), and they are inexpensive (the 24-quart size cost us $2.99; the 36-quart size $6.99). We put 3 or 4 quarts of warm water in the 36-quart canner and set the 24-quart inside it, double-boiler style. The 24-quart canner holds 4 or more gallons of milk, is not too deep to cut the curd with a long-bladed knife (such as a bread knife), and it is easily handled. The investment in these pots is about $10, and we use them at canning time to process tomatoes, peaches and other acid fruits and vegetables.

A Strainer — A piece of cheesecloth will do, but a colander or large sieve is convenient. You can improvise one by punching small holes in the sides and bottom of a one-gallon, restaurant-size can.

A Thermometer — A floating dairy thermometer works fine, but almost any thermometer that can be immersed can be used.

A Spoon — The handle must be long enough to reach to the bottom of the container.

8

A Knife — Same as above.

Cheesecloth — You'll need about one yard for wrapping, another yard for straining. It costs 10 to 15 cents a yard.

Bricks — You'll need 6 to 8 average-size bricks, which weigh about 4 pounds each. Rocks or other weights will do.

Paraffin — to coat hard cheese to prevent overdrying and mold growth. Buy a one-pound package.

THE INGREDIENTS

Milk — Goats' milk or cows' milk, raw or pasteurized. Whole milk makes the richest cheese, but skimmed or partially-skimmed milk can be used. One gallon of milk will make about one pound of hard cheese, slightly more soft cheese or about one quart of cottage cheese.

Starter — Some type of starter is necessary to develop the proper amount of acid for good cheese flavor. The kind of starter may vary according to your taste for cheese. You can buy buttermilk, yogurt or a commercial powdered cheese starter, or you may make a tart homemade starter by holding two cups of fresh milk at room temperature for 12 to 24 hours, or until it clabbers. A more complicated, but much more mellow starter may be made by adding ⅛ cake of yeast to 1 cup of warm milk and letting it stand 24 hours. Then pour out one-half of it and add 1 cup of warm milk. Every day for the next 7 days, pour off half the mixture and add 1 cup of warm milk. Keep in a warm place. At the end of a week, add the mixture to 2 cups of warm milk and let stand 24 hours. This is a cultured starter and it is now ready to use. If you make cheese regularly — we find our refrigerator filling up with milk about once a week — save 2 cups of clabbered milk from each batch of cheese just before you begin the Heating the Curd step. Keep it covered in the refrigerator for no more than one week.

Rennet — Rennet is a commercial product made from the lining of young animals' stomachs. The enzyme action of rennet causes the milk to coagulate in less than an hour, making the curd formation more predictable for cheesemaking. Rennet is available in extract or tablet form from drug, grocery or dairy supply stores. You can buy it in health food stores or in the special cheese/wine-making sections of gourmet food shops. Or you may order it by mail from American Supply House, P.O. Box 1114, Columbia, Missouri 65201 and Chr. Hansen Laboratory, Inc. Ask for a catalog.

Because natural rennet is of animal origin, many vegetarians prefer not to use it in making cheese. For that reason, a new, all-vegetable rennet is available in health food stores. But Grandmother made cheese without rennet *of any kind.*

To do so, let the milk clabber until a firm curd forms and the whey begins to separate, then proceed with the directions at the Cutting the Curd stage. Some people prefer the taste and texture of cottage cheese made without rennet, but in very warm weather you'll have to watch out that the milk doesn't spoil before it clabbers, and in winter weather it may take a long time to clabber.

Cheese Color — If you like your cheese a bright orange color you'll have to add cheese color, which also is available from American Supply House. We prefer our cheese its natural, creamy-white color.

Salt — After you've made cheese a few times, you'll learn the exact amount of salt that suits your taste, but some salt is needed for best flavor. Our recipes call for a minimum amount. You can use ordinary table salt, but flake salt is absorbed faster. Morton flake salt is available in some grocery stores.

BASIC DIRECTIONS

THE MILK   Use fresh, good quality milk from animals free from disease or udder infections. Either cows' or goats' milk may be used for any of these recipes, but it is very important *not* to use milk from any animal that has been treated with an antibiotic for at least three days after the last treatment. A very small quantity of antibiotic in the milk will keep the acid from developing during the cheesemaking process.

The milk may be raw or pasteurized, held in the refrigerator for several days or used fresh from the animal. It must be warmed to room temperature, then held until it has developed some lactic acid (ripened) before you start to make the cheese. You want it only slightly acid tasting. More acid develops as the cheese is made.

It is best to use a mixture of evening and morning milk. Cool the evening milk to a temperature of 60 degrees and hold it at that temperature overnight. Otherwise it may develop too much acid. Cool the morning milk to 60 degrees before mixing with the evening milk.

If you use only morning milk cool it to 60 or 70 degrees and ripen it three or four hours before beginning the first step, Ripening the Milk. Otherwise it may not develop enough acid to produce the desired flavor and may have a weak body.

If you are milking one cow or only a few goats, you probably will save a mixture of morning and evening milk in the refrigerator until you have a surplus of three or four gallons to make cheese.

When you are ready to make the cheese, select 10 or 12 quarts of your very best milk — remember that poor quality milk makes poor quality cheese — and warm it over a pan of warm water to 86 degrees. Stir it occasionally, so it doesn't skim over and so that it warms evenly.

BASIC DIRECTIONS FOR HARD CHEESE

RIPENING THE MILK

With the milk at 86 degrees add 2 cups starter, stirring thoroughly for two minutes to be sure it is well incorporated into the milk. Cover and let set in a warm place, perhaps overnight. In the morning taste the milk. If it has a slightly acid taste it is ready for the next step.

If you are not using rennet skip the next step and let the milk set 18 to 24 hours more, or until curd has formed and whey is separating.

ADDING THE RENNET

With the milk at room temperature add ½ teaspoon rennet liquid or 1 rennet tablet dissolved in ½ cup cool water. Stir for two minutes to mix the rennet in thoroughly. Cover the container and let it remain undisturbed until the milk has coagulated, for about 30 to 45 minutes.

CUTTING THE CURD

When the curd is firm and a small amount of whey appears on the surface the curd is ready to be cut. With a clean knife slice the curd into half-inch cubes by slicing through it every half inch lengthwise. Then slant the knife as much as possible and cut crosswise in the opposite direction. Stir the curd carefully with a wooden spoon or paddle and cut any cubes which do not conform to size. Stir carefully to prevent breaking the pieces of curd.

HEATING THE CURD Place the container in a larger one of warm water, double boiler style, and heat the curds and whey slowly at the rate of two degrees every five minutes. Heat to a temperature of 100 degrees in 30 to 40 minutes, then hold at this temperature until the curd has developed the desired firmness. Keep stirring gently to keep the cubes of curd from sticking together and forming lumps. As it becomes firmer the curd will need less stirring to keep it from lumping.

Test the curd for firmness by squeezing a small handful gently, then releasing it quickly. If it breaks apart easily and shows very little tendency to stick together it is ready. The curd should reach this stage 1½ to 2½ hours after you added the rennet to the milk.

It is very important that the curd be firm enough when you remove the whey. If it is not the cheese may have a weak pasty body and may develop a sour or undesirable flavor. If it is too firm the cheese will be dry and weak flavored.

When it is ready remove the container from the warm water.

REMOVING THE WHEY

Pour the curd and whey into a large container which you have lined with cheesecloth. Then lift the cheesecloth with the curds inside and let it drain in a colander or large strainer. A one-gallon can with drain holes is convenient for this step.

When most of the whey has drained off take out of the cheesecloth, put the curd in a container and tilt it several times to remove any whey that drains from the curd. Stir occasionally to keep the curd as free from lumps as possible.

Stir the curd or work it with your hands to keep the curds separated. When it has cooled to 90 degrees and has a rubbery texture that squeaks when you chew a small piece it is ready to be salted.

Be sure to save the whey. It is very nutritious and is relished by livestock and household pets. We save the whey for our chickens and pigs, but many people enjoy drinking it or cooking with it.

SALTING THE CURD

Sprinkle 1 to 2 tablespoons flake salt evenly throughout the curd and mix it in well. As soon as the salt has dissolved and you are sure the curd has cooled to 85 degrees, spoon the curd into the cheese form which has been lined, sides and bottom, with cheesecloth. Be sure the curd has cooled to 85 degrees.

15

PRESSING THE CURD

After you have filled the cheese form with the curd, place a circle of cheesecloth on top. Then insert the wooden follower and put the cheese form in the cheese press, if you have made one. If not, insert the follower and place weights on it.

Start with a weight of 3 or 4 bricks for 10 minutes, remove the follower and drain off any whey that has collected inside the can. Then replace the follower and add one brick at a time until you have 6 or 8 bricks pressing the cheese. When it has been under this much pressure for an hour, the cheese should be ready to dress. Pressing is extremely important, and if you want a hard, dry cheese, you'll need 30 or more pounds pressure for a 2½ to 3 pound cheese.

DRESSING THE CHEESE

Remove the weights and follower and turn the cheese form upside down so the cheese will drop. You may have to tug at the cheesecloth to get it started. Remove the cheesecloth from the cheese and dip cheese in warm water to remove any fat from the surface. With your fingers, smooth over any small holes or tears to make a smooth surface. Wipe dry.

Now cut a piece of cheesecloth two inches wider than the cheese is thick, and long enough to wrap around it with a slight overlap. Roll the cheese tightly, using two round circles of cheesecloth to cover the ends.

Replace the cheese in the cheese form, insert the follower and press with the 6 to 8 bricks another 18 to 24 hours. (Remember, these are general instructions, to be used for hard cheeses with the longest keeping qualities. Follow specific directions for pressing times in each recipe.)

DRYING THE CHEESE At the end of the pressing time, remove the cheese, take off the bandage, wipe the cheese with a clean, dry cloth and check for any openings or cracks. Wash the cheese in hot water or whey for a firm rind. Seal the holes by dipping the cheese in warm water and smoothing with your fingers or a table knife.

Then put the cheese on a shelf in a cool, dry place. Turn and wipe it daily until the surface feels dry and the rind has started to form. This takes from 3 to 5 days.

PARAFFINING THE CHEESE Heat ½ pound paraffin to 210 degrees in a pie pan or disposable aluminum pan deep enough to immerse half the cheese at one time. Be sure to heat the paraffin over hot water — never over direct heat.

Hold the cheese in the hot paraffin for about 10 seconds. Remove and let harden a minute or two, then immerse the other half. Check to be sure the surface is covered completely.

CURING THE CHEESE Now put the cheese back on the shelf to cure. Turn it daily. Wash and sun the shelf once a week. After about six weeks of curing at a temperature of 40 to 60 degrees the cheese will have a firm body and a mild flavor. Cheese with a sharp flavor requires three to five months or longer curing. The lower the temperature the longer the time required.

It's a good idea to test your first cheese for flavor from time to time during the curing period. One way is to cut the cheese into four equal parts before paraffining and use one of the pieces for tasting.

How long to cure depends on individual taste. As a rule Colby is aged 30 to 90 days and Cheddar 6 months or more. Romano is cured at least 5 months. Other cheeses are cured sometimes no more than two or three weeks. The cooler the temperature in the curing room the longer it takes to ripen. Once you have the temperature and time to suit your taste you will know exactly when your cheese will be ready.

RECIPES FOR HARD CHEESE

COLBY To make a small Colby cheese add 3 tablespoons starter to 1 gallon lukewarm milk. Let stand overnight to clabber, then proceed with Basic Directions through the Heating the Curd step.

When the curd is heated to the point where it no longer shows a tendency to stick together remove the container from the heat and let it stand one hour, stirring every five minutes.

Now proceed with the next following step, which is Removing the Whey, in the Basic Directions. After pressing the curd for 18 hours the cheese may be dried a day or two and used as a soft cheese spread or ripened for 30 days.

CHEDDAR There are several ways to make Cheddar. To make my version follow the Basic Directions through Removing the Whey. Then place the cubes of heated curd in a colander and heat to 100 degrees. This may be done in the oven or in a double boiler arrangement with two pots on top of the stove. It is important to keep the temperature between 95 and 100 degrees for 1½ hours.

After the first 20 to 30 minutes the curd will form a solid mass. Then it should be sliced into 1-inch strips which must be turned every 15 minutes for even drying. Hold these strips at 100 degrees for 1 hour. Then remove from the heat and proceed with Basic Directions, beginning at Salting the Curd. Cure for six months.

19

MOZZARELLA Mozzarella is a delicate, semi-hard Italian cheese which is not cured but is used fresh. It often is used in Italian dishes.

Follow Basic Directions, omitting Adding the Color, and proceed to Cutting the Curd. Instead of cutting the curd with a knife, break it up with your hands. Heat the curd as hot as your hands can stand. Then stir and crumble it until the curds are firm enough to squeak.

Proceed with Basic Directions at Removing the Whey and continue to Dressing the Cheese. At this point remove the pressed cheese from the cheese form and discard cheesecloth wrapping. Set the cheese in the whey which has been heated to 180 degrees. Cover the container and let stand until cool.

When cool remove the cheese from the whey and let drain for 24 hours. The cheese is now ready to eat or use in recipes.

CANTAL Cantal is a hard, yellow cheese with a sharp flavor and a firm texture. To make it follow Basic Directions through Pressing the Curd. Then remove the cheese from the cheese form, wipe off and allow to cure 24 hours.

The cheese is now broken into small pieces and 2 tablespoons of salt are worked in with the hands. After thorough kneading, it is again put in the cheese form and pressed 48 hours. Proceed with Basic Directions, omitting Paraffining the Cheese. Cure 3 to 6 months. While curing the cheese should be washed every three or four days with salt water (¼ cup salt to 1 quart warm water).

ROMANO   Romano is a hard, rather granular Italian cheese often used for grating. Unlike other hard cheeses, skimmed milk may be used.

Follow Basic Directions to Heating the Curd. At this point heat the cut curd slowly to 118 degrees and hold it at that temperature, stirring occasionally until the curd is quite firm (you can tell by touch or by tasting.) Then proceed with Basic Directions to Pressing the Curd. Follow directions, pressing it 18 hours. When removed from the cheese form the cheese is immersed in salt brine (¼ cup salt dissolved in 1 quart warm water), and let stand two to three hours. During the first stages of the curing process salt is rubbed on the surface. For a real Italian Romano appearance color the paraffin black (with crayon) and rub the surface on the paraffined cheese with olive oil at the end of the curing process period.

Romano is cured for 5 to 8 months for slicing and 1 to 2 years for grating.

TELEMÉ   Teleme is a pickled cheese made from goats' or ewes' milk. To make it follow Basic Directions past Pressing the Curd, but omitting the step of Salting the Curd. Press the curd one to two hours, then remove from the cheese form, cut into cubes and immerse in salt brine (¼ cup salt dissolved in 1 quart warm water). Leave covered in the brine 24 hours. The cubes then are drained, wiped dry and again pressed in the cheese form for 18 hours. The cheese is cured in diluted salt brine (¼ cup salt to 2 quarts water), 8 to 10 days. The cured cheese is white and creamy.

LONGHORN Add 2 cups starter to 1½ gallons warm raw milk. Cover and set in a warm place 12 to 24 hours or until thick and clabbered. Follow Basic Directions at Heating the Curd through Pressing the Cheese, omitting Salting the Curd. Remove cheese from the press, add 4 tablespoons butter and ¾ teaspoon baking soda. Chop until curd is quite fine and the butter and soda are thoroughly mixed in.

Press mixture down into a bowl or crock and let stand in a warm place 2½ hours. Then put the curds into a double boiler with 2/3 cup thick, sour cream and 1¼ teaspoon salt and heat slowly. As it begins to heat stir until all ingredients melt into one mass. Then pour into a well-greased bowl and allow to cool. It is ready to eat as soon as it is cold, but may be cured two to three months.

FETA Feta is a white, pickled cheese made from goats' or ewes' milk. It is not cured. To make this salt-cured cheese follow Basic Directions through Cutting the Curd. In the next step the curd is heated to no more than 95 degrees and drained when less firm than most hard cheeses.

In the next step, Removing the Whey, the curds and whey are poured into a cloth bag which is hung 48 hours until the cheese is firm. Feta is not pressed in a cheese form. When firm the curd is sliced and sprinkled with dry salt which is worked in with the hands. The cheese is then returned to the cloth bag which is twisted and worked to expel most of the whey and firm the cheese. After 24 hours, the cheese is wiped off and placed on a shelf to form a rind. It is ready to eat in three to four days.

RECIPES FOR SOFT CHEESE

Soft cheeses usually are mild and aged little, if at all. The keeping qualities are not as good as hard cheeses. Soft cheeses are not paraffined, but are wrapped in wax paper and stored in the refrigerator until used. Except for a few soft cheeses that are aged, they should be eaten within a week or two for best flavor.

The simplest soft cheese is fresh curds, which Grandmother made by setting fresh warm milk in the sun until the curds separated from the whey. The most familiar soft cheese is cream cheese which is made by draining curds for a few minutes in a cloth bag.

If you gather from this that the making of soft cheese is not nearly as complicated as hard cheese, you're right. Here are some of the simplest recipes:

SWEET CHEESE

Bring 1 gallon of whole milk to a boil. Cool to lukewarm and add 1 pint of buttermilk and 3 well-beaten eggs. Stir gently one minute, then let set until a firm clabber forms. Drain in a cloth bag until firm. The cheese is ready to eat in 12 hours.

CREAM CHEESE

Add 1 cup starter to 2 cups warm milk and let set 24 hours. Add to 2 quarts warm milk and let clabber another 24 hours. Warm over hot water 30 minutes, then pour into a cloth bag to drain. Let set one hour. Salt to taste and wrap in waxed paper. May be used immediately for sandwiches, on crackers or in recipes calling for cream cheese. Refrigerate until used.

OR

To 1 quart of thick, sour cream add 1 tablespoon salt. Place in a drain bag and hang in a cool place to drain 3 days.

ENGLISH CREAM CHEESE

Pour 1 quart of cream in the top of a double boiler. Add hot water to bottom pan. Heat the cream slowly almost to the boiling point. Remove from heat and add 1 rennet tablet dissolved in 1 tablespoon cold milk. Stir well and let stand until thick, then break slightly with a spoon and pour into a drain bag. Let drain 24 hours, then press in a cheese press under light weight for 24 hours. Remove from press, wrap in cheesecloth and rub flake salt over the cloth. Hang to dry 1 or 2 days before slicing.

NEUFCHATEL

Cool 1 gallon freshly-drawn milk or heat refrigerated milk to 75 degrees. Add 1/3 cup sour milk or starter. Stir for one minute, then add half a rennet tablet dissolved in a quarter cup cool water. Stir again for one minute. Let set undisturbed in a warm place (about 75 degrees) for 18 hours.

At the end of that time dip off the whey on the surface of the curd. Then dip the curd into a cheesecloth bag and hang in a cool place to drain. When the curd appears dry place in a bowl and salt to taste. Mix in salt thoroughly.

Ladle the salted curd into a cheesecloth-lined cheese form, press smooth with a spoon and top with a layer of cheesecloth. Insert the wooden follower and apply pressure (6 bricks). The length of time required to press the cheese into a cake suitable for slicing varies according to the temperature, the amount of moisture and the weight applied, but is usually from 45 minutes to 1½ hours. When the cheese is firm enough to cut it is ready to eat. It is best fresh but will keep a week or more in the refrigerator.

POTATO CHEESE

Potato cheese is made from cows', goats' or ewes' milk. The curd is made from sour milk or with rennet. Potatoes are peeled, boiled and mashed or put through a sieve, then added to the curd in various proportions such as 2 parts potatoes to 3 parts curd. Salt and caraway seed are added to taste. The mixture is dried three to four days, then mixed again and placed in a cheese form for 24 hours. The cheese is removed from the press when firm. Cure it two weeks.

MONT D 'OR   Whole or partially skimmed milk is set with rennet at 90 to 100 degrees, cut and pressed in a cheese form. The cheese is salted on the surface and eaten without curing.

SCAMORZE   Scamorze is a soft, whole milk cheese which is eaten fresh. To make it cream skimmed from the evening milk is mixed with the whole morning milk and warmed to 98 degrees. The milk is then cooled to 80 degrees, starter is added and rennet is mixed in thoroughly. When set the curd is cut into half-inch cubes and heated until the curd settles to the bottom of the container. The whey is poured off and the curd is drained until firm. The whey then is heated to 122 degrees and poured back over the curd, which is kneaded and stretched until it is smooth and cohesive and will form long threads when stretched. The temperature is kept at 140 degrees. The curd then is cut into small slices and the whey heated to 180 degrees. The whey then is poured over the cubes of curd and the curd is kneaded and pressed with a paddle while immersed in the whey. Again it is stretched by hand or with the paddle until it is very elastic. The cheese is divided into round balls the size of lemons and these are dropped into hot whey. As they cool, the cheeses are shaped by hand. When the whey is cold the cheeses are dipped in salt water (¼ cup salt to 1 quart water), and dried a few hours, then stored in the refrigerator until use.

RIESENGEBIRGE   Riesengebirge is a soft cheese made from goats' milk which is coagulated with rennet at about 90 degrees. The curd is broken up, the whey dipped off and the curd set to drain in a warm place in the cheese form for 24 hours. The cheese is then removed from the form, salted on the surface, dried 3 or 4 days and set in the refrigerator to cure a week or two. Wrap and store in the refrigerator until eaten.

KRUTT CHEESE

Krutt is made by clabbering skimmed milk, adding salt, then hanging the curd in a cloth bag to drain. It sometimes is pressed for one to two hours. Then small balls are formed by hand. These are dried in the sun, all afternoon, then stored in the refrigerator. It is best eaten within a week.

GAISKASLI

Gaiskasli is a soft cheese usually made from goats' milk. The fresh milk is set with enough rennet to coagulate it in 40 minutes. The curd is then broken up, stirred and dipped into small tin cans which have the bottoms and sides perforated with holes. The cans are set on a rack so the cheese curd can drain freely and salt is sprinkled on top. After two days, the cheeses are removed from the cans, re-inserted top-end first in the cans and sprinkled with salt again. This cheese cures in about three weeks in the refrigerator.

SCHMIERKÄSE Pour 4 quarts boiling water into 4 quarts thick, sour milk. Let stand for a moment, then turn into a drain bag and hang aside overnight. When ready to serve beat well, season with salt and pepper and add cream to taste. Serve as a spoon cheese or make into:

CHEESE BALLS To each pint of drained curd add 2 ounces melted butter, 1 teaspoon salt, a dash of pepper and 2 tablespoons thick cream. Work together until smooth and soft. Make into small balls to serve with salad.

PARMESAN BALLS Put ½ pint drained curd into a bowl. Rub with the back of a spoon until smooth. Add 2 tablespoons grated Parmesan cheese, 2 tablespoons melted butter, a half teaspoon salt and a dash of red pepper. Mix well and roll into balls. Chill well.

PROCESSED CHEESE Use freshly-pressed or aged cheese. Grind in a food grinder, using fine blade. In a double boiler mix 5 cups ground cheese, 1 teaspoon soda, 2 teaspoons salt, ½ cup butter and 1½ cups milk. Cook over boiling water until cheese melts into sauce and makes a soft "processed" cheese, which can be sliced for sandwiches. For a softer spreading cheese, add more milk.

PROCESSED PIMIENTO CHEESE To each 2 cups of the above processed cheese add ¼ cup fresh or canned chopped pimiento.

CHEESE SPREAD

Let 2½ gallons skimmed milk sour until thick. Heat very slowly until hot to the touch. Do not allow to boil. Hold at this temperature until the curds and whey separate. Strain through cheesecloth and allow curds to cool a little, then crumble with the hands. Makes 4 cups crumbled cheese. Let set at room temperature 2 to 3 days to age.

To the 4 cups crumbled curds add 2 teaspoons soda and mix in with the hands. Let set 30 minutes. Add 1½ cups warm milk, 2 teaspoons salt and 1/3 cup butter. Set over boiling water and heat to the boiling point, stirring vigorously. Add 1 cup cream or milk, a little at a time, stirring after each addition. Cook until smooth. Stir occasionally until cold. Makes 1½ quarts cheese spread.

FLAVORED CHEESE SPREADS

To 1 cup of the above cheese spread add 3 tablespoons crumbled bits of crisply fried bacon, *OR* 1 tablespoon chopped chives, *OR* 4 tablespoons chopped, drained pineapple.

GERMAN CHEESE

Put 2 gallons of clabbered milk in an iron pot over low heat and bring it to 180 degrees in 45 minutes. Drain off the whey and put curds in a colander. When the curds are cool enough to handle, press with the hands to extract any remaining whey. The warmer you work it the better. Put the drained curd in a dish and add 2 teaspoons soda and 1 teaspoon salt, working in well with the hands. Press curd with the hands to form a loaf. Let set 1 hour, when it will have risen and be ready to slice. Will keep several days in a cool place. If the cheese is dry and crumbly it may have been heated too much or pressed too long. If it is soft and sticky it was not heated enough or pressed enough.

EGG CHEESE

Over medium heat bring 1 gallon of sweet milk to a boil. Meanwhile, in a bowl beat 6 eggs well, then add 2 cups of clabbered milk and ½ teaspoon salt. Add this mixture to the milk which has come to a boil and again bring to a boil. When the milk and eggs separate, pour into a drain bag and hang to drain for several hours. May be eaten after 8 to 10 hours.

OR

To 2 gallons of clabbered milk, add 1 gallon sweet milk and 6 well beaten eggs. Salt to taste and heat over a low fire until it curdles. Drain for several hours, then press in a cheese press 24 hours. Slice to serve.

DUTCH CHEESE

Set a pan of curded milk on the back of a wood burning stove and let heat very slowly until the curd is separated from the whey. Drain off the whey and pour the curd into a drain bag. Hang and let drain 24 hours. Chop ball of curd and pound until smooth with a potato masher or round-end glass. Add cream and butter, salt and pepper to taste. Make into small balls, or press in a dish and slice to serve.

POTTED CHEESE Cheese that has dried out or begun to mold can be made into a sandwich spread and preserved on the pantry shelf by cutting away any mold and grating the dry cheese with a fine grater. Then, using a potato masher or the bottom of a smooth glass, pound smooth, gradually adding one ounce of sherry, 1 tablespoon of butter and 1 teaspoon of sugar to each pound of cheese. Spoon the smooth paste into small jelly glasses and pour hot paraffin over the top to seal. Store in a cool, dry place two weeks before using. Will keep several months.

COTTAGE CHEESE Bring 1 gallon whole or skimmed milk to 75 to 80 degrees and add 1 cup starter. Cover and set in a warm place 12 to 24 hours or until a firm clabber forms and a little whey appears on the surface.

When a clabber is formed cut into half-inch cubes by passing a long knife through it lengthwise and crosswise. Then set the container in a larger pot containing warm water. Warm the curd to 110 degrees, stirring often to keep it from sticking together. Be careful that you do not overheat.

When the curd reaches the proper temperature taste it from time to time to test for firmness. When it feels firm enough to your liking, (some people like their cottage cheese rather soft; others quite firm and granular) immediately pour into a colander lined with cheesecloth, and drain for two minutes. Lift cheesecloth from the colander and hold under tepid water, gradually running it colder, to rinse off the whey. Place the chilled curd in a dish, add salt and cream to taste and chill thoroughly before serving.

Cottage cheese may be eaten as a spoon cheese or strained (or put through a blender) and used as a low calorie dip or in recipes calling for sour cream. It is best eaten as soon as it is chilled, but will keep up to one week in the refrigerator.

Homemade cottage cheese does not contain preservatives, so it does not keep as long as the commercial variety usually does.

OR

Add 1 cup starter to 1 gallon freshly-drawn milk. Cover and set in a warm place overnight. In the morning add half a rennet tablet dissolved in a half cup water. Stir one minute. Cover again and let stand undisturbed for 45 minutes. Cut curd into half-inch cubes and set container in a larger pot of warm water and warm the curd to 102 degrees. Proceed as in first recipe.

OR

Add 1 cup starter to 2 gallons warm skimmed milk. Stir well and pour into a large roaster pan with a lid. Place in a warm (90 degree) oven (heat off) overnight or about 12 hours. In the morning take out 1 pint of the clabbered milk and refrigerate it to use as a starter for the next batch. Turn on oven and set at 100 degrees. Heat clabber in oven 1 hour, then cut into half-inch cubes. Do not stir or move pan unnecessarily. Leave milk in oven until curds and whey are well separated. When curd rises to the top of the whey turn heat off and let set until cool. Dip off excess whey and dip curds into a cheesecloth-lined colander to drain. Pour curds into a dish and add salt and cream to taste.

OR

Heat 1 quart sour milk in the upper part of a double boiler over hot water. Heat until lukewarm, then line a large strainer with cheesecloth dipped in hot water and pour in the milk. Over the strainer pour 1 quart warm water. When the water has drained off, pour another quart of warm water over the milk. Repeat. When the water has drained off for the third time, gather the ends of the cheesecloth to form a bag and hang to drain overnight. Add salt to taste.

OR

Pour 2 quarts clabbered milk into a large pan. Into it slowly pour boiling water, continuing until the curds start to form in the milk. Let set until the curds may be skimmed from the top. Mix curds with cream and salt lightly.

SWEET MILK COTTAGE CHEESE

Heat 2 quarts milk to lukewarm. Dissolve 2 rennet tablets in 2 tablespoons cold water and add to milk. Stir two minutes. Let stand undisturbed in a warm place until set, about 1 hour. Pour into a drain bag and let drain 3 to 4 hours. Remove from bag and break into fine pieces. Moisten with cream and season with salt and pepper to taste.

SOUR MILK COTTAGE CHEESE

Pour 2 quarts sour milk into a double boiler. Heat over warm water until soft curd is formed. Pour into a drain bag and let drain. After 3 to 4 hours remove cheese from bag, break into pieces and moisten with cream. Season with salt and pepper.

COTTAGE CHEESE WITHOUT HEATING

Add 1 teaspoon salt and 1 crushed, dissolved rennet tablet to 1 quart lukewarm sweet milk. Stir thoroughly. Let stand in a warm place until set. Beat with a fork to break the curd, then turn into a drain bag and let hang until the liquid has drained from the curd. Moisten with cream and season with pepper.

OTHER MILK RECIPES

TO MAKE CULTURED CHEESE STARTER
Add ⅛ yeast cake to 1 cup warm milk. Let stand covered in a warm place for 24 hours. Then pour off half the liquid and add 1 cup warm milk. Each day for 7 days pour off half the liquid and add 1 cup warm milk. On the seventh day do not drain off any but add 2 cups warm milk. Let set another 24 hours and you have 3 cups cultured cheese (or yogurt) starter.

TO MAKE CULTURED BUTTERMILK
Warm raw milk to 90 degrees, then add 1 cup cultured (from the grocery store) buttermilk for each quart of warm milk. Stir well, cover and let set in a warm place overnight or in the sun 3 or 4 hours. Reserve 1 cup for the next batch.

BUTTERMILK DELDA
Bring 2 quarts buttermilk to a boil and add 4 tablespoons honey. Moisten 4 tablespoons flour with sweet milk and add to the simmering buttermilk, stirring until thick. To be eaten warm or cold.

BROWN WHEY CHEESE
After making cottage cheese, put the whey over low heat to simmer until it reaches the consistency of thick cream. Remove, stir and store in small glass jars in the refrigerator. Spread on bread or crackers or use as a dressing on salad.

WHEY LEMONADE
Strain 1 quart whey left after making cheese. Add 6 tablespoons sugar and the juice of 2 lemons. Chill.

TO MAKE YOGURT

Making yogurt essentially is the same as making cheese starter or cultured buttermilk. The milk is warmed to 100 to 110 degrees, the culture is added and the mixture is kept at the desired temperature for several hours. At about 100 degrees you can make yogurt in 5 to 6 hours, but you can leave it 10 to 12 hours if you like a tarter flavor.

It is important to keep the mixture at the proper temperature for the necessary length of time in order to allow the culture to develop. If you have a yogurt maker you simply follow the manufacturer's directions. If you don't, use your ingenuity:

With a Thermos — Almost fill a thermos (preferably wide mouth) bottle with warm (100 degrees) milk. Add 2 tablespoons plain yogurt and mix thoroughly. Put the lid on and wrap the thermos in two or three terry towels. Then set in a warm, draft-free place overnight. (On winter nights, over the furnace register is a good place.)

In an Oven — Pour 1 quart warm milk in a casserole dish and add 3 tablespoons plain yogurt. Stir well and cover casserole. Place in a warm (100 degree) oven with the heat off. Let set overnight.

On a Heating Pad — Set an electric heating pad at medium temperature and place in the bottom of a cardboard box with a lid. (A large shoe box works well.) Fill small plastic containers with warm milk, add yogurt starter to each and mix well. Put on lids. Wrap heating pad around containers as much as possible, then cover with towels to fill box. Put lid on box and let set undisturbed for 5 or 6 hours.

In the Sun — Pour warmed milk into a glass-lidded bowl or casserole. Add yogurt starter and cover with the glass lid or a clear glass pie plate. Place in the sun on a warm (not too hot) summer day and let set 4 or 5 hours. Watch it to make sure it isn't shaded as the sun moves.

On the Back of the Stove — Grandmother made her "clabber" by setting a bowl of freshly-drawn milk on the back of the stove after supper. She added 1 cup of starter to each 2 quarts of milk and let it set, loosely covered with a dish towel, on the back of the cooling wood range overnight. If you are fortunate enough to have a wood range in your kitchen this method works beautifully.

TO SKIM MILK

If you don't have a cream separator or don't want your milk completely skimmed you may use this method of partially-skimming milk:

Cool milk immediately after milking; then pour through a milk filter into a large, open mixing bowl. Refrigerate uncovered for 12 to 24 hours. At the end of that time take a large spoon and skim off the thick, leathery cream which has risen to the top. It comes off easily. Spoon it into a pint jar, cover it and refrigerate. Add to the jar each day. It will keep well in the refrigerator for one week.

What you skim off by this method is only a part of the cream, which leaves the milk rich tasting yet will give you about 1 quart of cream a week from 2 gallons of milk a day. You could get more with a cream separator, but unless you're separating several gallons a day it takes more time to clean the separator than the extra cream is worth.

WAYS TO PRESERVE MILK

FREEZING   During the summer months when the grass is lush and green and our milk pail runneth over we freeze some milk for winter use. We use the half-gallon size dairy milk cartons, which our city friends save for us in exchange for a few fresh country eggs. We fill them almost to the fold mark and staple the tops shut. If used within a month or two the milk is almost as good as fresh. After that time it tends to curdle and separate, which affects the texture, but not the taste. Sometimes we run it through the blender and drink it, but usually we drink what fresh milk we get and cook with the thawed frozen milk.

CANNING   Wash and rinse pint canning jars. Immerse them in hot water and bring to a boil. Cover and boil 10 minutes. Fill hot jars within 1 inch of the top with milk which has been heated to just below the boiling point. Be careful, since milk scorches easily. Top jars with caps according to manufacturer's directions and place in a hot water canning kettle (not a pressure canner). Pour warm water over the jars, being sure the water is at least two inches above the tops of the jars. Keep water boiling three hours. At the end of that time turn heat off and allow water to cool somewhat before removing jars. While canner is processing keep extra boiling water on the stove to replace any boiled away in the canner. Keep boiling water two inches deep over jars at all times.

Canned milk will keep over the winter. It tastes somewhat like condensed milk only it's not as thick. Canned goats' milk may have a "goaty" flavor.

MAKING BUTTER

Butter may be made from sweet or sour cream in a variety of equipment ranging from an electric mixer or blender to a plain glass jar with a tight-fitting lid.

If you make butter often, you may want to buy a churn — a simple piece of equipment designed for making butter. They vary from the large, old-fashioned wooden barrel churns which will accommodate up to five gallons of cream to the small, glass-jarred, wooden-paddled churns that are still sold by Sears, Roebuck in hand-operated or electric models.

Sweet cream butter takes longer to churn and, if the cream is very fresh it may take several hours to turn to butter. Sour cream churns into butter in 30 to 35 minutes. Either sweet or sour cream churns quicker if it has been aged two to three days in the refrigerator. Sweet cream butter is sometimes preferred for its mellow, bland flavor. Sour cream butter has a richer taste.

Below are two recipes for butter. One is a recipe for churning sweet cream in an electric mixer. The other calls for ripened cream which is churned in an old-fashioned churn.

SWEET CREAM BUTTER

Pour the cold, heavy cream into a chilled mixing bowl. If you make butter once a week from the cream accumulated during the week it will give the cream time to ripen a little, which improves the taste and makes it easier to whip. Or leave the cream a day or two at room temperature until it begins to clabber.

Turn the mixer slowly to high speed and let the cream go through the stages of whipped cream, stiff whipped cream and finally two separate products — butter and buttermilk. In a churn, turn slowly for 15 to 20 minutes. It is only during the last stage, as the butter separates from the buttermilk, that the process needs attention. Then you must turn the speed to low or it will spatter wildly. When the separation has taken place pour off the buttermilk. (Save it. It's great for making biscuits or pancakes or to drink. The yield is 1¼ to 1½ lbs. of butter and 1 to 1¼ quarts of buttermilk).

Now knead the soft butter with a wet wooden spoon or a rubber scraper to force out all the milk, pouring the milk off as you knead. When you have all the milk out refill the bowl with ice water and continue kneading to wash the remaining milk from the butter. (Any milk left in will cause the butter to spoil.) Pour off the water and repeat until the water is clear.

You now have sweet butter. If you want it salted, add a teaspoon of flake salt. Uncolored butter may be an appetizing creamy-white color, but if you want it bright yellow, you may add butter color. (You can order it from

American Supply House too.) To help your family make the transition of taste and color you can add a half pound of margarine to 1 pound of homemade butter, then gradually decrease the amount of margarine each week.

One quart of well-separated, heavy cream makes about 1 pound of butter.

SOUR CREAM BUTTER

Ripen cream by adding ¼ cup starter to each quart of heavy cream. Let set at room temperature 24 hours, stirring occasionally. Chill the ripened cream two to three hours before churning.

When it is chilled, pour the cream into a wooden barrel or glass jar churn. If you wish to, add butter coloring at this point. Keep the cream and the churn cool and turn the mechanism with a moderately fast, uniform motion. About 30 to 35 minutes of churning usually will bring butter, but the age of the cream, the temperature and whether the cream is from a morning or a night milking will affect the length of time required.

When the butter is in grains the size of wheat, draw off the buttermilk and add very cold water. Churn slowly for one minute, then draw off the water.

Remove the butter to a wooden bowl and sprinkle it with 2 tablespoons flake salt to each pound of butter. Let stand a few minutes, then work with a wooden paddle to work out any remaining buttermilk or water and mix in the salt. Taste. If the butter is too salty, wash with cold water. If it needs it, add more salt.

While working, keep the butter cold. If it should become too soft during hot weather, chill the butter until hardened before finishing.

INDEX

44

NOTES